From BATTLEFIELI

FRODSHAM AUX
MILITARY HOSF
1915 – 1919

by

Arthur R Smith

A Short History – containing a remarkable collection of previously unpublished photographs

World War 1 Centenary Edition

FROM BATTLEFIELD TO BLIGHTY

FRODSHAM AUXILIARY MILITARY HOSPITAL 1915 – 1919

by

Arthur R Smith

ISBN 978-0-9932428-0-9

First published by Avid Publications – 2001
This edition published by Frodsham Town Council – 2015

Front cover: Recruiting Poster for Voluntary Aid Detachments
Reproduced courtesy of Imperial War Museum, London

Frontispiece and back cover: Nurses and Patients at
Frodsham Auxiliary Military Hospital Circa 1916

FOREWORD

It is a matter of some surprise that in the various historical accounts of bygone Frodsham, slight reference is made to the Frodsham Auxiliary Military Hospital, which was established on Overton Hill in 1915. Indeed, it is difficult to think of any event in the town's long history that is more worthy of note. Between 1915 and 1919, over 3,400 wounded servicemen from all over the Empire were nursed back to health with the help of many local people, who also offered friendship and provided the soldiers with opportunities for leisure and entertainment.

For some years, Arthur Smith has been adding to our knowledge of the local historical scene with his publications dealing with various aspects of Frodsham's past. His latest research throws light on a proud and honourable, but little known period in the history of the town.

In order to illustrate his book, the author has used many recently-discovered unique and striking photographs. As usual, he has explored in depth to present his investigation in some detail.

This book is an influential memoir because it is the first to chronicle important events, which were fading in the public memory.

We are indebted to Arthur Smith for this work, which will give much satisfaction to all those who are interested in the history of our area.

H F Starkey

March 2001

Acknowledgements

My thanks are due to the many people who have kindly supplied me with information for this history over quite a long period.

Top of the list come Tony and Mona Harding, who allowed me to use the late Dorothea Urmson's collection of photographs and for their invaluable help in many other ways.

Secondly, I wish to thank Joan Taylor for all her special help and encouragement.

Next, I am much indebted to the following people who have given me various details about the hospital: John and Margaret Adams, Margaret Blythe, Edgar Brereton, Rowland and Janice Edmonds, Eric Ellison, Les Finnerty, Jean Forster, Mary Gold, Rhoda Haughton, Kate Hill, Christine and Brian Lloyd, Tom Nicholls, David Nield, Dilys O'Neill, Walter Ormsby, Bernard Price, John and Sheila Scully, Judith Shore, Mrs Willis (of Helsby), Les Worrall and Lance Yates.

I owe a great debt of gratitude to Mr H F Starkey for his helpful advice and encouraging comments; and to Stuart Crook for his unstinting assistance with copying the photographs and with preparation of the text on the computer.

Also, I wish to record my sincere thanks to the staff of the public institutions who have responded to my letters and sent me valuable information, in particular, the staff of Cheshire Record Office, St John's Ambulance Association, British Red Cross and British Medical Association.

I hope this short history helps to put on record the devoted service of the volunteers and the professionals who organised and staffed the Frodsham hospital and provided a haven for some of those who were wounded in the First World War.

Finally, I would like to mention the late Trevor Smith who shared his wide knowledge of the hospital with me and told many anecdotes about the staff. It was his stories that gave me the initial inspiration to undertake this line of research.

Arthur Smith

March 2001

CONTENTS

Introduction

This is an account of the auxiliary military hospital established in Frodsham, Cheshire during the First World War. From March 1915 sick and wounded men from many different regiments were looked after at Bellemonte, Overton, which is situated on the slopes of Frodsham Hill. By the time the hospital finally closed its doors on 15 September 1919, 3,435 patients had been treated there.

The Frodsham hospital was one of hundreds of such voluntary institutions set up in the early years of the Great War. In these days of a comprehensive National Health Service, it is difficult to imagine how much reliance was once placed on voluntary effort, without which the returning wounded would have fared very badly. Often, the staff of these hospitals was drawn from Voluntary Aid Detachments established in the years immediately prior to 1914.

Despite these preparations, no one could have imagined the appalling scale of the casualties in the 1914-18 War, which was beyond all previous experience. For example, in the South African War, after three years of fighting, 21,157 men were wounded, whereas in 1916 alone the total number of wounded arriving in this country was 523,153.

As more evidence has come to light and the story pieced together, three main features of the Frodsham hospital have become apparent. Firstly, the considerable scale of public support for the venture; secondly, the admirable efficiency and dedication of the managers, doctors and nursing staff, many of whom were volunteers; and thirdly, the relative speed with which most of the patients were rehabilitated.

By 1918, the auxiliary hospital at Overton was one of the largest of its kind in the country. Only two others – the Haigh Lawn at Altrincham and the hospital at Bromborough – had nearly as many beds. From all accounts, Frodsham's had become a spacious, well-equipped and efficient hospital. As far as the evidence allows us to judge, it was a proud chapter in Frodsham's history.

Chapter 1 — Founding of the Hospital

Origins of the Project

By December 1914 rumours abounded that Frodsham was to have its own auxiliary military hospital. Many preparations went on behind the scenes until finally the hospital opened to patients on 4 March 1915 in a rather unusual location. It was decided that the single-storey roller-skating rink at Overton, erected in 1912 on land behind the Bellemonte Hotel, could be easily converted to provide suitable accommodation for wounded soldiers.

The original idea to raise money for the conversion of the skating rink had been put forward shortly after the outbreak of the war. The owner of the premises, Mrs Parker Hoose, had been approached and she had agreed to loan the building for this purpose. Interested townspeople formed a committee and between £600 and £700 was quickly subscribed. Local tradesmen loyally gave support and volunteered assistance towards equipping the room. Hopes were suddenly dashed when it was learnt that the government might require the use of the premises for other purposes. However, according to a report in the *Chester Chronicle* of 23 January 1915, the committee was soon informed that the authorities had no plans to use the building and that the premises could be made into a temporary hospital. The report goes on to state that during the following week the committee met several times to put the work in hand immediately and that Messrs Lea of Runcorn were instructed to fit heating apparatus. The writer concludes, 'the work will now proceed apace, so that the building will be ready in about three weeks time ...."

The building did not need much conversion as it consisted of a large skating hall with a fine wooden floor, which had been kept in a polished condition. In fact, this sprung maple floor was regarded as ideal for hospital purposes.

Viewing Day and Official Opening

On 3 March 1915 a viewing day was held, when members of the public were invited to look around the new hospital. Admission took the form of a gift-in-kind. About 1,500 people came and it is estimated that gift parcels amounted to over £35, which would be worth many times more than that sum today. In the afternoon everyone gathered in the main hall and Mr J J Crosfield, who was a director of Crosfield's Soap Works at Warrington and Chairman of the Board of Management of the hospital, gave an introductory address. He thanked people for their generous response in the initial stage of the venture and appealed to the people of Frodsham for their continued support. He hoped it would be regarded as an opportunity to “do something for our soldiers who were doing so much for us”. Mrs Thomas then declared the hospital officially open.

Frodsham Auxiliary Military Hospital: View from the rear of the Bellemonte Hotel, showing the ingenious construction of the roof with its five arches to give a large open floor space. The entrance hall can just be seen in the centre of the picture and the matron's residence on the extreme right.

Frodsham Auxiliary Military Hospital: View from Overton Village. On the left is the Pump Cottage and across the road is Hawthorne Cottage, both of which were demolished many years ago. Note the pathways on the hillside, up and down which the more able patients would have walked many times.

Military Hospitals in the UK

At the outbreak of the First World War hospital accommodation in the UK consisted of 7,000 equipped beds, of which 2,000 were in use. By the time of the Armistice in November 1918 the number of beds had increased to over 364,000. This vast increase had been achieved in a variety of ways: additions were made to existing military hospitals; new hospitals constructed; Territorial Force general hospitals opened and enlarged; special war hospitals established in asylums, Poor Law institutions and other public buildings; places found for the wounded in civil hospitals and, finally, a large number of auxiliary hospitals opened. These latter institutions were established and equipped by voluntary organisations and private individuals. As a matter of fact, Cheshire led the way in the provision of auxiliary hospitals. According to the Annual Report of the Cheshire Branch of the British Red Cross Society for 1919, there were 60 auxiliary hospitals in the country by the summer of 1915. By the end of 1918 the figure had reached 85. As the following table shows, most of these were organised by the British Red Cross:

British Red Cross	76
Order of St John	4
Civil Infirmaries	2
Joint Committee of Red Cross and St John	1
Independent	2

Frodsham was one of the independent institutions. Although it had this independent (or private) status, after 1916 all auxiliary hospitals which were in receipt of a War Office capitation grant came under the jurisdiction of the County Director. These 85 hospitals provided a grand total of 4,533 beds. In proportion to its population, as mentioned earlier, Cheshire had a larger number of auxiliary hospitals and beds than any other county. The total number of patients treated in its hospitals under the jurisdiction of the County Director from October 1914 to the final demobilisation in 1919 amounted to 74,412 (exclusive of out-patients).

Mr T Stanley Bower

Before the opening of the Frodsham Auxiliary Military Hospital the Board of Management had appointed Mr T Stanley Bower of Overton Hall, Five Crosses, Frodsham as the Officer-in-Charge. In this role he was responsible for administration, discipline and maintenance of the hospital, whereas it was the duty of the Matron to oversee the wards and the nursing staff. She was responsible to the Medical Officer for the patients.

Almost certainly Mr Bower relied on a small team of volunteers to serve as administrative staff. In due course the Board received a War Office capitation allowance for every patient being treated at the hospital. In addition certain items (for example, the uniforms worn by patients) would be supplied by the War Office.

THE MEDICAL OFFICER

Shortly after the outbreak of war, Dr William Edward Burton volunteered for service with the Royal Army Medical Core. In March 1915 he was appointed as the Medical Officer at the Frodsham hospital. Captain Burton had qualified with LSA London in 1889 and as MRCS Eng in 1891.

Captain Burton (back row, 5th from left) with nurses and patients.

In the summer of 1916 he was succeeded by Dr Harold Blades Ellison but continued to help at the hospital whenever needed. Dr Ellison MA MB resided at 'Brentwood', Red Lane, Frodsham. He served as the Medical Officer until late in 1917. Dr Ellison, whose family lived in Hoylake, came to Frodsham in 1912 to join Dr Burton's practice.

VISITING TIMES

Visiting days were Wednesdays from 2 pm to 4 pm and Sundays from 4 pm to 6 pm. Opportunities to visit patients must have been in considerable demand as it was soon decided to regulate the numbers by means of permits. Permits could be obtained from Mr R H Dutton, the Honorary Treasurer, at Parr's bank, Main Street, Frodsham. In the early summer of 1915 Mr Bower requested that local residents with motor cars and gardens consider placing them at the disposal of the wounded soldiers in the hospital from time to time.

Mrs Brown (first Matron), Dr Ellison, Sister Davies (2nd from right), two other Sisters (back row, right) and volunteer nurses. Mrs Brown served at the hospital from March 1915 until the summer of 1917.

Local people with patients whom they have befriended.

Chapter 2 — The Hospital Buildings

Skating Rink

In late Victorian times there were two sets of attractions on Frodsham Hill: Manley View Recreation Grounds and, the less well known, Bellemonte Picnic and Pleasure Grounds. In 1865 Robert Briscoe had opened the first tea-room at Mersey View. Slowly, over the next 30 or 40 years, more attractions were added until, by the end of the century, not only had the tea-room been considerably enlarged, but parents and children enjoyed the swing boats, the donkey rides and games on the green. Mersey View had become a Mecca for family and Sunday School outings.

In 1908 Mrs Parker-Hoose, who had inherited the Recreation Grounds, gave orders for the helter-skelter to be constructed. It soon proved to be worth every penny of the £300 which it cost to build as children from miles around enjoyed its thrilling slide. By the year 1912 roller-skating had become a fashionable pastime and, in the same enterprising vein, she opened the skating rink as a further attraction at Bellemonte Picnic and Pleasure Grounds.

These grounds, about six acres in extent, were situated to the rear of the Bellemonte public house and consisted of a bowling green, a croquet lawn, a gymnasium, archery butts and a small dancing room, some of which can be seen on the map below:

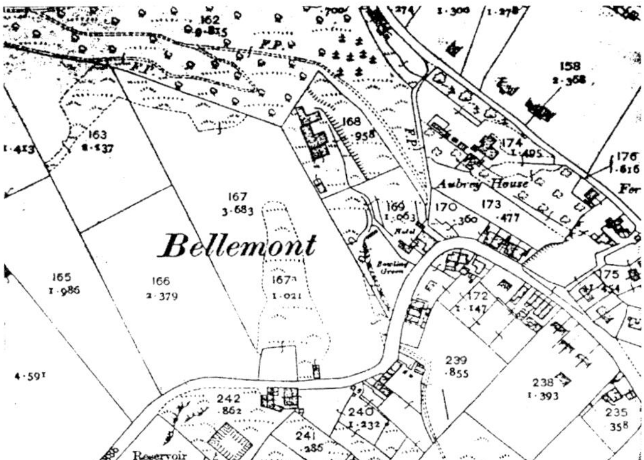

A section of the 1910 Ordnance Survey Map of Frodsham, showing the Bellemonte Hotel and the bowling green with the gymnasium and dancing room on the land to the rear.

The roller skating rink proved very popular, especially with parents and children. Older residents can remember many stories about the happy times their parents and grandparents enjoyed there. As stated earlier, Mrs Parker-Hoose lent these premises early in 1915 when the urgent need for more military hospitals arose.

A beautifully drawn poster, probably dating from the early 1900s – before the days of the skating rink – advertising the various attractions at the Bellemonte Picnic Ground.

Gradual Expansion

When the hospital opened in March 1915, it had just 30 beds in the main hall but soon 20 more were added. Later, in the same year, a further 20 were brought into use, filling the existing single room. This original area became known as Ward I.

Pressed by the military authorities to extend the accommodation, the Board decided to order the construction of a long wooden hut, which would provide room for an additional 50 beds. This building was completed in December 1915 – the cost being met through the generosity of local subscribers. By Christmas that year, there were 80 patients in the hospital.

In March 1917 there were 130 beds in the two wards, including six in a verandah for open-air treatment. At this point the managers arranged for a further 40 beds to be provided in tents, but later in the year it was decided that accommodation in tents was impractical, and they were returned to the Army. Next, the Board proposed to increase the verandah-type of accommodation to provide a further 26 – 30 beds. To accomplish this, they gave instructions in August 1917 for another new building to be erected – a special feature being its glass-panelled doors, which could be opened wide to allow in plenty of fresh air and sunlight. Those concerned with the finances must have been relieved to hear that the cost of this new development would not fall on the Board of Managers as the money had been donated.

In this way, the hospital was gradually enlarged until, as we have seen, it had accommodation for a total of 160 beds, although in 1918 the average number of in-patients resident daily was only 125.

Thus, in its final form, the hospital comprised a main ward which could hold up to 70 beds, two subsidiary wards (the wooden hut and the new building of August 1917), an operating theatre, a dining area and kitchen, a recreation room and a number of stores. The three wards and the other rooms are shown in the plan on the next page.

Plan of the F.A.M.H. Site 1918/1919

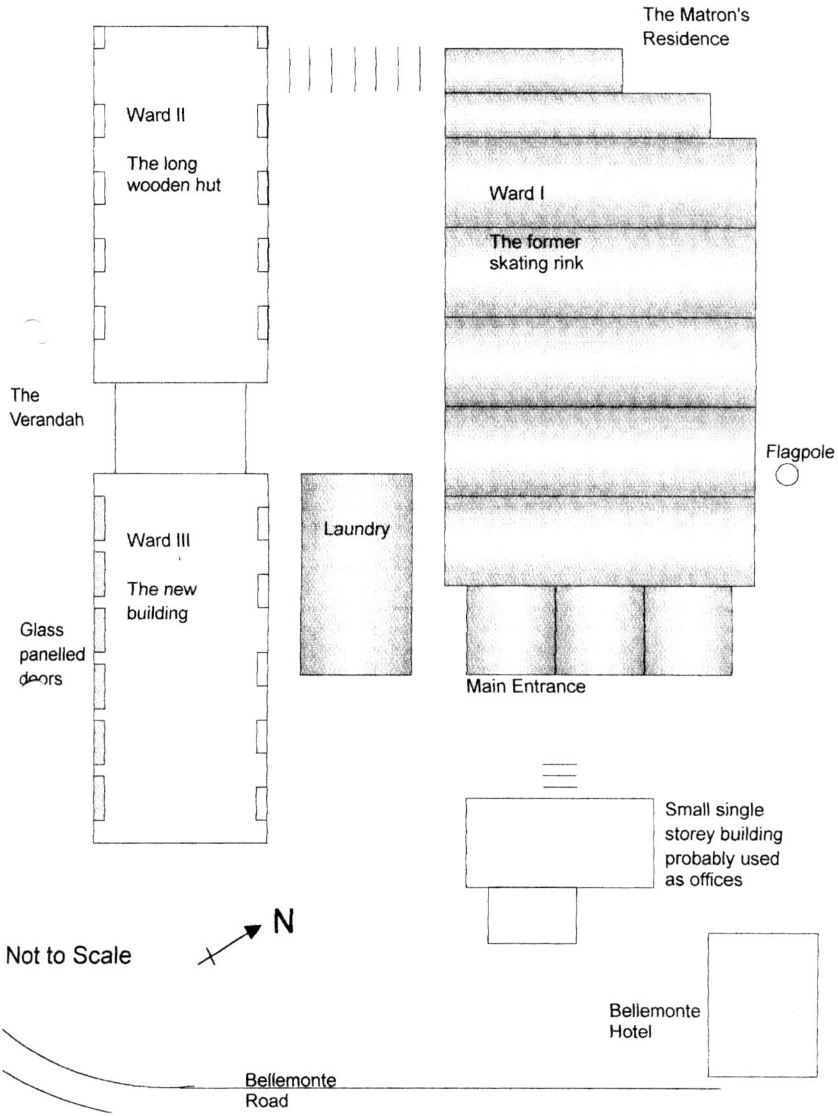

Plan of Frodsham Auxiliary Military Hospital Site 1917/18.

The Main Hall in 1915, showing how the beds were set-out in double rows to accommodate the growing number of patients.

Early in 1916, extra accommodation was provided by the addition of a long wooden hut (known as Ward II). This building stood on the hillside behind the main hall.

New building constructed in August 1917 (left) and the main part of the hospital (Ward I) is between the two white buildings.

Another view of the new building showing the glass-panelled doors open wide to allow plenty of fresh air and light.

The entrance to Ward I is on the extreme right.

The balcony or verandah between Ward II and Ward III in January 1919
Patients from left: Pte Lewis, Cpl Spencer, Pte Cockcroft and Pte Wilson. These four men slept in this room.
Sister Davies is holding the dog (right), Nurse Urmson – with her efficiency stripe, awarded for long service and experience, on her sleeve – is standing to the right of Pte Wilson.

Two of the patients in front of entrance to Ward I.

The Bellemonte Hotel in 2001.

It was built in 1872 by James Rigby, who sold it in 1897 to Mrs Parker-Hoose. Its licensee at the time of the Frodsham Auxiliary Military Hospital was Wilfred Sampson.

As the photographs show, the new building proved to be a big improvement on Ward II. The large glass-panelled doors could be opened wide in the summer time, making it easy for beds to be brought out on to the field. The hospital authorities commented that the advantage of this would be to make better use of the spare beds. At the same time the severe cases would benefit enormously by the open-air treatment. With this additional space, the total number of beds had now reached 160. Eventually, more beds were added in existing wards until, by 1918, the total number had reached 190 – making Frodsham one of the largest hospitals in the country.

Chapter 3 – The Medical and Nursing Staff

Dr Ellison, MA MB

According to the Medical Register, Dr Ellison qualified MRCS LRCP in 1908 and MB BCh in 1910 (Camb and Liverpool). Later that year he became the Gynaecological House Surgeon and House Physician at the Royal Infirmary, Liverpool. As mentioned earlier, he moved to Frodsham in 1912 to work with Dr Burton as a family doctor. During 1915 he assisted at the newly established hospital at Overton, but early in the New Year he volunteered for service in the Royal Army Medical Core (RAMC) and was posted to a field station in Northern France. After many months of intensive medical and surgical work behind the front line, he was sent back to England. In the summer of 1916 he took up an appointment as the Medical officer at the Frodsham Auxiliary Military Hospital. During the next few months he worked extremely hard to cope with the increasing number of casualties who were being sent to Overton.

Dr Ellison and Mrs Brown (first Matron) in deck-chairs with some of the nurses and soldiers. Picture taken in early days of the hospital before uniforms were issued to patients.

Dr Ellison resigned his position in August 1917, when he received his recall to the RAMC. He was succeeded as the Medical officer by Dr Adams. After the war, Dr Ellison resumed his work as a general practitioner. During the many years that he served as a doctor in Frodsham, he was noted for his good humour and his generosity towards his less well-off patients. Often he would ignore the matter of payment for his services.

He lived at 'Brentwood', Red Lane, and later at 'Thornhill', Fluin Lane, Frodsham. In retirement, he moved to 9A Park Road, West Kirby, Wirral. He died in 1959, aged 79.

DR ALFRED ADAMS

Starting his medical career later than most, Dr Adams qualified MB BCh with honours at Liverpool University in 1910. Two years later he took his MD and the Diploma in Public Health. He held the Johnston Colonial Fellowship in Pathology and Bacteriology at Liverpool for a year before being appointed the Medical Superintendent of the Liverpool Sanatorium, Delamere Forest in 1912. He remained in this post, except for a break during his military service, until he retired in 1938. Dr Adams was, in many ways, a pioneer in the early institutional treatment of pulmonary tuberculosis, and conducted the difficult work of the Sanatorium with great skill and initiative.

In the First World War he served in the RAMC, with the rank of Captain, in France, Gallipoli and Salonika and, in the latter, as in-charge of the No 2 Mobile Bacteriological Laboratory. After this service abroad he returned to England – probably through injury or ill health. It was at this point that he became the Medical Officer at the Frodsham Auxiliary Military Hospital.

When the hospital closed in September 1919, he resumed his full time post at the Liverpool Sanatorium. In the latter part of his life, Dr Adams lived at 15 Woodvale Road, Knutsford where he died, after a short illness, in January 1943.

DR SELBY MBE

Dr Thomas James Selby, who for many years had a surgery at The Rock, Main Street (now High Street), Frodsham, also served as Medical Officer at the Frodsham Auxiliary Military Hospital. He had gained his MB at the University of Durham in 1892 and his LRCP and LRCS at Edinburgh. After the war he became the Medical Officer of the National Children's Home at Newton Hall, Frodsham and held a similar position at the Poor Law Hospital of the Runcorn Union. At a later date, he was awarded the MBE. He retired to the Lake District and lived at Wordsworth House, Cockermouth.

THE NURSES

The number of nurses serving at the hospital gradually increased until, by 1918, there were 23, including the Matron. As one would expect, there was an acute shortage of nurses in all types of hospitals during the First World War. With the dreadful carnage on the Western Front and thousands of casualties returning home, there was soon a desperate need for more hospitals and more nurses. Many volunteers were recruited. They were known as VADs – the Voluntary Aid Detachment nurses. After a very short training, they were thrown into the hard and difficult work of tending the sick and wounded. Often frowned upon by the trained nurses, unpaid and over-worked, they were among the true heroines of the War. As far as we know, most of the ordinary nurses at the Frodsham hospital were VADs.

Mr Stanley Bower with doctors and nursing staff in 1918.
2nd Row, From Left: Dr Adams, Mr Bowers, Matron and Dr Selby.
3rd Row, From Left: Sister Mather (3rd) and Sister Davies (4th).

VOLUNTARY AID DETACHMENTS (VADS)

In the years immediately before the outbreak of the War, VADs were established in many towns and villages under the auspices of Red Cross and St John's Ambulance Association. Shortly after the opening of hostilities, the War Office recommended that these Detachments be utilised for service with RAMC. Members of these VADs were to serve in military hospitals when RAMC personnel were called to the front. In other places they were called upon to staff the auxiliary hospitals. An example of this type of arrangements was the Red Cross hospital establishment at Helsby, Cheshire in 1915. The hospital was set up at the Britannia Recreation Hall and staffed by No 72 Helsby Women's Detachment with Mrs Eva Horner serving as Commandant. Orderlies and transport services were provided by No 13 Men's Detachment – Commandant: Mr F S Horner. Mr and Mrs Horner lived at Gorsefield, Helsby.

As will be seen from the figures given below, Red Cross played a considerable part in nursing the wounded. In the first year of the War, the volunteer nurses, cooks, kitchen maids, clerks, ward maids, laundresses and motor drivers who staffed the hospitals in Cheshire, came from 78 Red Cross VADs (65 Women's and 13 Men's) with personnel of some 2,300. By the end of 1918, the total number of VADs working in the country had reached 113 (97 Red Cross and 16 St John's). Of these, 89 were Women's and 19 were Men's Detachments – five being Transport Units, for which both men and women were eligible. The number of War Office brassards (badges) issued to members of mobilised VADs totalled 5,918 and the estimated number of personnel directly employed in connection with the sick and wounded about 8,000. Rather remarkably, the Overton hospital did not fit exactly into this pattern because it was organised independently and there was no VAD in Frodsham for it to draw upon.

The nearest St John's VADs were at Winsford and Chester, and the nearest Red Cross units at Helsby, Chester, Northwich and Warrington. VAD nurses were expected to hold current first-aid and home-nursing certificates. Each course took six weeks and, almost certainly, the nurses at Overton would have been trained by Red Cross or St John's Ambulance Association through one of the neighbouring detachments mentioned above, or they would have served a probationary period in a local hospital. It should be remembered that none of the VAD nurses in any district were paid or given a uniform allowance except in special circumstances. (See Appendix III for how VAD units were established in Kent before the War and then used to staff the newly organised auxiliary hospitals in that county.)

Although it had an independent status, the Frodsham Auxiliary Military Hospital came under the general jurisdiction of the War Office. For this purpose, initially it was affiliated to the 1st Western General Hospital, Liverpool; but later transferred to the War Hospital, Cheshire.

MISS WINIFRED DAVIES

The actual credentials of only one VAD nurse at Overton have come to light. The late Mrs Freda Bailey, nee Miss Winifred Davies, was enrolled as a Special Probationer of St John's Detachment 1130 of West Lancashire on 6 November 1918 as shown in the certificate below. As far as we know, Miss Davies served at the Overton hospital until its closure in December 1919.

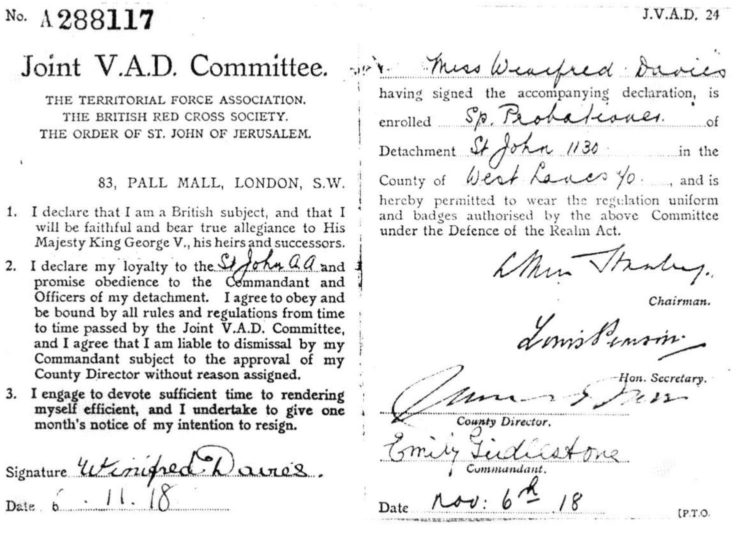
No. A288117

J.V.A.D. 24

Joint V.A.D. Committee.

THE TERRITORIAL FORCE ASSOCIATION.
THE BRITISH RED CROSS SOCIETY.
THE ORDER OF ST. JOHN OF JERUSALEM.

83, PALL MALL, LONDON, S.W.

1. I declare that I am a British subject, and that I will be faithful and bear true allegiance to His Majesty King George V., his heirs and successors.
2. I declare my loyalty to the St John A.A. and promise obedience to the Commandant and Officers of my detachment. I agree to obey and be bound by all rules and regulations from time to time passed by the Joint V.A.D. Committee, and I agree that I am liable to dismissal by my Commandant subject to the approval of my County Director without reason assigned.
3. I engage to devote sufficient time to rendering myself efficient, and I undertake to give one month's notice of my intention to resign.

Signature Winifred Davies.

Date 6. 11. 18

Miss Winifred Davies. having signed the accompanying declaration, is enrolled Sp. Probationer of Detachment St John 1130 in the County of West Lancs 40, and is hereby permitted to wear the regulation uniform and badges authorised by the above Committee under the Defence of the Realm Act.

Chairman.

Hon. Secretary.

County Director.

Emily Tiddlestone
Commandant.

Date Nov: 6th 18

[P.T.O.

Miss Davies' Certificate of Enrolment in the West Lancs VAD.

There are no grounds for believing that any Queen Alexandra Nurses – the corps of specialist nurses set up for the Army – ever served at the hospital. However, the Matron and four or more Sisters who were employed would be trained nurses. This small staff of professional nurses was assisted by the numerous volunteers.

ST JOHN'S AMBULANCE BRIGADE

Members of St John's Ambulance Brigade worked as orderlies and stretcher-bearers. They met the trains carrying the wounded at Chester station and conveyed the men to the various hospitals. At their destination, the Ambulance Corps did just whatever they were told to do to help the doctors and nurses give comfort to their patients. Usually this meant they undressed, bathed and fed the soldiers and, in other ways, attended to their needs.

The following extract from the *Chester Chronicle* for Saturday 18 August 1917 illustrates the work of St John's Ambulance men:

> "On Monday evening the inmates of the auxiliary military hospital were increased by the arrival of 40 more wounded soldiers, all cot cases. The party consisted of men from various regiments, including four Canadians. The men had made a quick and comfortable journey from Northern France. They left Le Havre at 8am and arrived in Frodsham at 6.30pm, and were bedded down by 7.30pm. Local cars left the Town Hall at 5 pm accompanied by Messrs Powell, Clarke, Goodall, Patten and Jones of the local Ambulance Corps and under the charge of Commandant Bower."

According to another report in *Chester Chronicle* in November 1917, classes were being held at Frodsham Fire Station to increase the strength of the local Ambulance Corps. The report highlights the need for more trained personnel to deal with the new arrivals at the Overton hospital. The instructor at these classes was Dr Selby.

Members of the local St John's Ambulance Brigade with their wives and friends.
Front Row: Frederick William Booth (3rd from right) who contracted empyema whilst attending to patients at the hospital.
Back Row: Dr Selby (in white coat).

Elaborate decorations with the tree (right) at Christmas 1916 in Ward I.
Dr Ellison and Matron sitting on bench.

Christmas 1916 in Ward II – the long wooden hut.
The highly polished tables, chairs and floor suggest that perhaps, at times, this was more of a convalescent home than a hospital dealing with acute medical and surgical cases.

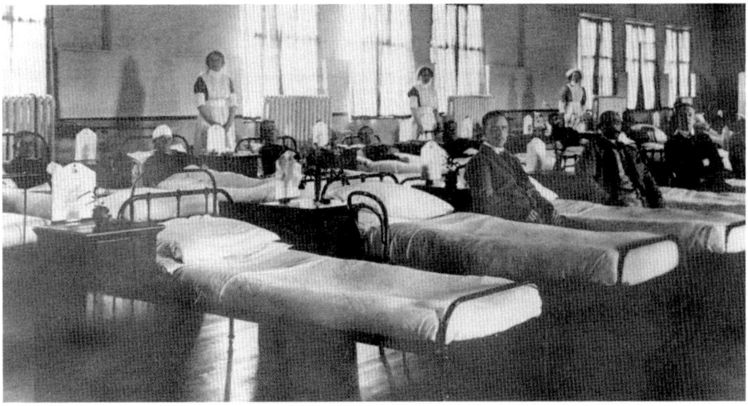

Ward I – Bed patients and convalescents with their nurses.

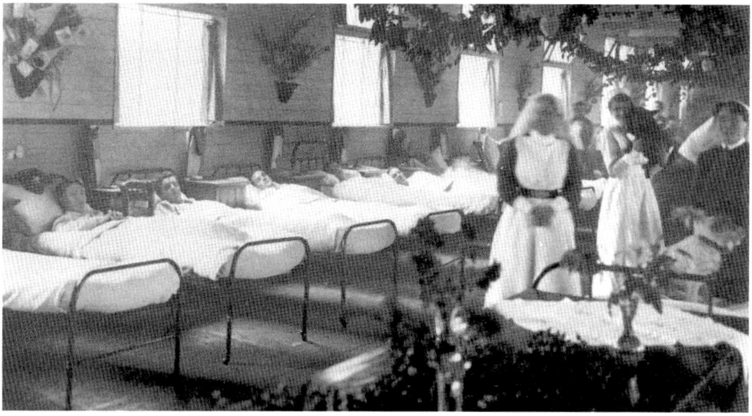

Christmas 1917 in Ward II.
Patients in bed (from left): Pte Nutting, Pte Leyland and Pte Peacock.
Right: Sister Mather, Nurse Campbell and Matron.

Dr Adams and Mrs B Stevens (new Matron) at the main entrance of the hospital.

Matron, with her dogs, outside her residence at the northern end of the hospital.

Christmas 1917 in Ward II.
Sister Mather (left) with Nurse Urmson (behind her).
Matron and Nurse Cameron (at the table).

Christmas Dinner – 1917.
This is the only photograph, which shows the main dining room.
(Note the billiard table in the foreground.)

Christmas 1918 in Ward III.
Sister Davies (centre) and Nurse De Silva (right) with patients.

Christmas 1918 in Ward III – Nurses and Patients.
Both this and the photograph on the previous page give a good view of the interior of Ward III.

A NURSE'S LIFE: DUTIES AND HARDSHIPS

If the working conditions in other military hospitals in those days are anything to go by, then almost certainly the nurses at Overton worked long hours – maybe 10 or 12 hours each day, probably starting at 7 or 7.30am. Then, every few weeks there would be night duty to face – a long stretch from 8pm to 8am. All manner of unpleasant tasks had to be undertaken, ranging from cleaning up serious wounds to supporting freshly amputated limbs whilst they were dressed and dealing with badly suppurating infections. Washing and bathing severely wounded patients would be no easy task, and constantly emptying bedpans and similar chores were not the pleasantest of jobs.

No doubt, many of the nurses faced a long journey to and from their work, which may have entailed walking a considerable distance. Certainly, some would have trekked from the bus stop in Main Street or from Frodsham railway station up the hill and back again every day. Pleasant enough in summer, perhaps, but not so enjoyable on cold and wet winter mornings and evenings. Conditions in the wards at Overton must have been unpleasant at times, especially in the hutted accommodation, where the only heating was provided by stoves. This must have left some parts of the rooms bitterly cold in winter and other parts warm, but maybe full of fumes. In hot weather, these wooden huts would become unbearably stuffy. No doubt, this is the reason why some of the photographs show patients lying in their beds in the open air.

"THE TESTAMENT OF YOUTH"

One of the few accounts of a VAD nurse in the First World War is contained in Vera Brittain's book, 'The Testament of Youth'. Unfortunately, no such description by a Frodsham nurse has come to light – not even a few letters, or an extract from a diary. But, at least, we do have the evidence of the photographs. To help the reader imagine the probable background to some of these pictures, a few extracts from Vera Brittain's book are quoted below.

One could easily imagine that any one of the Frodsham nurses could have been in the following situation:

> "*When I began to work in the long hut, my duties consisted chiefly in preparing dressing-trays and supporting limbs – a task which the orderlies seldom undertook because they were so quickly upset by the butcher's-shop appearance of the uncovered wounds. Soon after I arrived I saw one of them, who was holding a basin, faint right on top of a patient." (p. 211)*

A more unexpected problem might well have arisen from the incessant playing of gramophone records in the wards. Probably, many of the soldiers at Overton enjoyed listening to the popular songs of the day such as '*If I were the only girl in the world*' or '*When Irish eyes are smiling*' but, as Vera Brittain says, the constant repetition of these songs may have been a source of considerable irritation to the nurses.

In the next extract, Vera Brittain describes how she felt about the preparations for Christmas at her military hospital in Camberwell. No doubt, the Frodsham nurses had similar experiences.

> "The night *before Christmas Eve I found my ward transformed into the gay semblance of a sixpenny bazaar with Union Jacks, paper streamers, crinkled tissue lampshades and Christmas texts and greetings, all carried out in staggering shades of orange and vivid scarlet and brilliant green. In the cheerful construction of red paper bags, which I filled with crackers and sweets for the men's Christmas stockings, I found that the hours passed quickly enough." (p. 234)*

Judging by the photographs of the wards at Christmas, the nurses and other helpers must have spent considerable time making dozens of streamers and garlands, and in decorating the walls with foliage. Also, no doubt, the Frodsham nurses 'filled brightly coloured paper bags with crackers and sweets for the men's Christmas stockings', and then felt a warm glow of benevolence when their patients woke early on Christmas morning and reached for their home-made presents.

Looking Behind-the-Scenes

Although the photographs constitute an almost unique visual record of life in an auxiliary hospital, they do inevitably present a somewhat sanitised view of what went on there. They are snapshots of happier moments, for example, of patients and nurses in neat and tidy wards at Christmas time, or outside on the field on a warm summer's day. Unfortunately, the photographs do not depict any of the less pleasant side of hospital life. In the whole collection of 150 photographs, there is no record (nor would one expect there to be in those times) of the nurses at work: dressing serious wounds, emptying bed-pans, changing sheets or scrubbing bed-mackintoshes, lifting patients, washing and bathing them and all the other countless tasks that they had to undertake in the course of a day's work.

Similarly, there is no record of the behind-the scenes work of the cooks and kitchen staff preparing hundreds of meals every day, and of the rest of the innumerable jobs that were essential to keeping everybody well-fed. For example, the planning of the meals, buying the foodstuffs, checking and carrying in the deliveries, cooking and serving the food and then, afterwards, the piles of plates, dishes and cutlery which had to be washed. Another big undertaking for the staff was the cleaning of the wards and the constant changing of bed linen. There is one photograph that shows a mound of sheets ready for the laundry but, with 190 beds, what a busy place that department must have been! And how on earth did they cope with all that drying – not to mention the ironing!

Then there was the general care-taking, keeping the boilers going for the radiator heating and supplying coal or coke for the stoves. Also, the daily routine of sweeping the floors, dusting and polishing the furniture.

When a convoy arrived with 30 or 40 new casualties, there were extra demands made on everyone's energies. The patients, some suffering from terrible injuries, had to be carefully washed and bathed, then dressings applied and hospital uniforms supplied. One should not forget one important fact lying behind all this: that the majority of the nurses were volunteers who gained very little financial reward for their labours.

A Sad Time

Unfortunately, one of the worst events that the nurses and doctors faced was the death of a patient. Such occasions were rare at Frodsham Auxiliary Military Hospital, but a few deaths did occur – as we shall see in a later chapter.

The first patient to die was Pte Alfred Carter. His funeral is described in some detail in the *Chester Chronicle* of Saturday 25 December 1915:

> *"Pte Carter of the 1st Lancashire Regiment who died at the Frodsham Military Hospital on Thursday last, was interred in the Overton churchyard with military honours on Tuesday."*

The report goes on to explain that Pte Carter had been at the front for 14 months when he fell sick. He had been brought to the hospital three weeks before but it had been necessary to perform an operation on him. Exactly why he died subsequently is not disclosed. The report continues:

> *"The procession from the hospital to the churchyard was led by a firing party composed of men from the Royal Field Artillery under Cpl Mallard. The coffin, which was covered with a Union Jack, was wheeled on a bier. The bearers were all patients at the hospital and were in the charge of Sgt Davies, formerly police constable at Kingsley, who had been wounded in the face, body and leg. The other bearers were Cpl Keife, Cpl Henderson, Privates Smith, Lefevre, Newsham, Barton, Massey and Newbury. The coffin was followed by the sister of the deceased and several members of the hospital staff, including Mrs Brown (Matron), Sisters Speak, Fraser, Green and Gaskell. In the procession were also Capt Barton – the Medical Officer of the hospital, Mr Bower – Superintendent, Dr Ellison and the following patients: Privates Manning, Rutter, Dobson, Robinson, Barton, Ravenshill, Diball, M Wood and L/Cpl James. At the entrance to the church and in the street, a large number of people had assembled and many followed the cortège into the church. It was the first military funeral from the hospital and it cast a gloom over the village of Overton. In the church and on the graveside, Reverend Myres officiated. After the service three volleys were fired over the grave and the 'Last Post' sounded."*

This poster was used to recruit VAD nurses for overseas service in 1915.
(Courtesy of Imperial War Museum)

Sister Davies (front),
Sister Mather,
Nurse Williamson
and
Miss Melhuish on a
workman's ladder.

Background:
Framework of the
new Ward III
August 1917.

Nurse De Silva (right -
with St John's Ambulance
Brigade armband).

Sisters and nurses enjoying a respite from their labours.

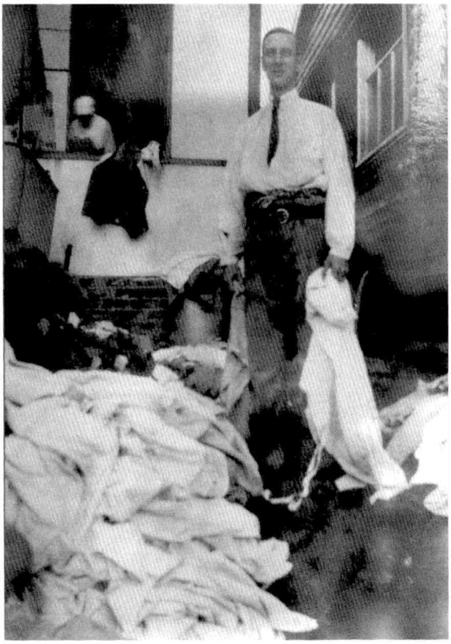

Sorting the laundry.

Some of the staff of Ward II in May 1918.

Top left to right: Nurses De Silva, Urmson and Galloway, Sister Mather and Nurse Campbell.

Nurse Urmson with colleagues from Ward II.

Back left to right:
Nurses Guile, Willis, Williamson and Campbell.

Seated at front:
Nurse De Silva.

Background:
Ward III – near side.

Two patients – equipped with walking sticks.

Background:
The 'Balcony' between Wards II and III.

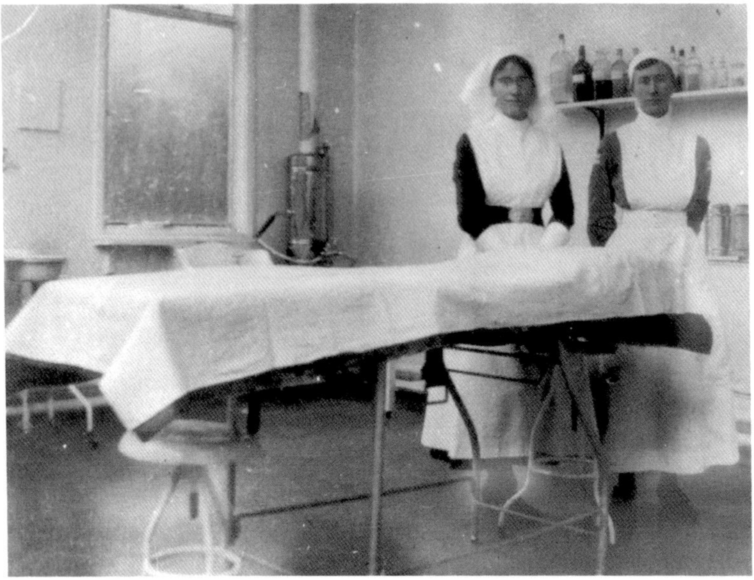

A Sister and a Nurse in the operating theatre.
Operations were carried out once a week, usually on Tuesdays.

An Orderly pauses for a few moments on his rounds with the dressings trolley.

Matron with 'Hughie'.
('Hughie' was, almost certainly, the District Nurse.)

Picnic on the hill for some of the nursing staff.
Foreground: Nurses Hickson and De Silva with Mr Bower.
(Could that be Mrs Parker-Hoose, standing at the back?)

Chapter 4 — PUBLIC SUPPORT

DONATIONS AND FUND-RAISING EVENTS

One of the most remarkable features of the story of Frodsham Auxiliary Military Hospital is the high level of public support for the venture. As we have seen, the original premises were made available by Mrs Parker-Hoose. Gifts poured in on the first Viewing Day, and the success of the whole enterprise was only made possible by generous public subscriptions. Many of the staff gave their services free. Most of the nurses were volunteers, the doctors often attended their patients free-of-charge and much of the administrative work was done without payment.

At the same time, the hospital received a relatively large sum in the form of a War Office capitation allowance with which it was able to meet the various bills for provisions, equipment (for example, new beds), medicine, drugs, surgical appliances, some salaries and wages, laundry and other miscellaneous expenses (see Appendix 1 – Accounts to December 1916). By 1916 the rate of capitation allowance had been raised to three shillings (15p in decimalised money) per patient per day. In addition to the public subscriptions, during the first six months of the hospital's existence, donations in kind continued to arrive almost daily. Over 20% of the patients' food and provisions were supplied through these gifts.

However, as the accounts demonstrate, over one-third of the hospital's income came from subscriptions and donations of one form or another. A small but nonetheless significant part of this income came from individual or schools' fund-raising efforts. In June 1915, Miss Linaker and Mrs N Linaker raised £14 by means of the Black Bag trick! Unfortunately, for today's fund -raisers, no details of the 'trick' are given, but it is interesting to learn in the same report how the managers spent this particular sum of money – on hot water bottles, cushions, dressing gowns, a chair and a collecting box.

On Wednesday 1 March 1916 pupils from 'The Close' private school at Overton raised £12 for the hospital with a performance of '*Scenes from Cranford*'. The proceeds were used to provide five garden seats for the ward tables.

The Ryder Boys staged a similar fund-raising event with a dramatic performance at the Drill Hall in Main Street, Frodsham at the end of October 1916. What a pity that we do not have any details of who these actors were or of what they performed! However, the venture must have been well attended as it raised over £89. In a letter to the organisers, the Honorary Secretary of the Board of Management of the hospital, Holman Kingdom expressed his grateful appreciation of the public support given to this event and his sincere thanks to the performers for their donation.

Towards the end of January 1917, the local branch of the Girls' Friendly Society held an entertainment in the Parish Rooms in aid of the hospital. A religious play called '*Mirror for Souls*' was performed and a good sum of money taken. According to a report in the *Chester Chronicle* for 11 August 1917, a series of functions were held during the weekend to augment the funds of the hospital. On Saturday evening, the local Subscription Band assisted by artists from other bands, gave an open-air concert in Main Street, Frodsham. Unfortunately, the details of the other events were not given.

A Midsummer Night's Dream

Later in August, 'The Close' School raised a further sum of over £44 with a performance of scenes from '*A Midsummer Night's Dream*'. The managers used some of this money to purchase three special adjustable wheel-chairs, six air cushions and six hot water bottles.

More Operations

In September 1915 it was reported that there had been comparatively few wounded soldiers coming in and, therefore, the expense of running the hospital was higher per head. Early in the following year greater numbers started to arrive and, by December, the total number of patients treated since March 1915 had reached 753.

Despite the local community's generous support, in the autumn of 1917 the managers were finding it difficult to make ends meet. As Mr J J Crosfield explained at the Annual General Meeting, the cost per patient per day was more than 50% greater than in the first year of the hospital. The reasons were two-fold: firstly, everything bought by the hospital had become more expensive and, secondly, the very serious cases now being sent to Frodsham entailed great additional expense. Some idea of the extent of this problem can be seen from the fact that there were 37 operations carried out in May.

Mr Crosfield went on to state that it was impossible to say what the cost would be in the future, but at least one shilling (5p in decimalised currency) per head per day beyond the Army allowance would be needed. For an average of 120 men per day, between £1,000 and £1,200 would be required during the next six months. Mr Crosfield thought that this was a large sum to find but he said: "*I am confident everybody sympathises with our wounded Tommies and will wish to help them through the work we do in this, our local hospital*".

Finally, he reminded his audience that subscriptions or donations would be most gratefully received by Mr R H Dutton, Honorary Treasurer of the Board of Management at Parr's Bank, Main Street, Frodsham. Also, that gifts in-kind should be sent to the Matron at the hospital.

"OUR DAY"

Another example of voluntary effort – this time probably of only indirect benefit to FAMH – is contained in a report in the *Frodsham Parish Magazine* for August 1918. On Saturday 10 August, local volunteers organised a special event in the town called 'Our Day' – to raise money to help the British Red Cross and the Order of St John to continue their work for the wounded soldiers. Members of the public were urged to purchase and wear little Red Cross Flags. The organisers expressed their surprise that there were some people who did not seem to be aware of the "*splendid work done by these two Societies for our wounded soldiers*". To enlighten these people, a specified showing of the film '*From No Man's Land To Blighty*' had been arranged at the Picture Palace in Chapel Lane at 8 pm on 9 August. The pictures would show how the wounded were brought in from the field, tended by doctors and nurses and sent home in Red Cross trains.

The report goes on to state that the main event of 'Our Day' will be a fête at Mersey View Pleasure Grounds on 10 August from 2.30 pm till 9 pm. The entertainment will include sports, palmistry, tennis, competitions, Aunt Sally, music, dancing and tea, with Frodsham Silver Band in attendance. The Marchioness of Cholmondeley had agreed to open the fête and Lady Brooke will be present.

Unfortunately, there is no mention in subsequent pages of how successful the event turned out to be and how much money was raised. But, undoubtedly, it was typical of the fund-raising ventures that enabled the Red Cross and the Order of St John to carry on with their important work.

J J CROSFIELD

From 1906 to 1915, Joseph John Crosfield, son of John Crosfield, along with his brother, George, ran the family firm of Crosfield Ltd, soap manufacturers of Warrington. By 1914 they employed about 3,000 people, of whom 500 were women.

In 1892, the 26-year-old Joseph Crosfield had married Alice Lilian, only daughter of Oliver Stokes Stack of Lansdown Crescent, London. Her father had been the District Superintendent of the Bengal Police. They were married at Christ Church, Paddington, and they decided to settle in Frodsham. They lived at 'Netherdale', Carriage Drive – at the foot of Frodsham Hill.

Joseph was fond of cycling long distances – no doubt through Delamere Forest and on to Tarporley and Beeston – but his wife could not keep up. So he bought a tandem, but soon discovered this meant he did most of the hard work, so he invested in a BSA motorbike.

They had two sons, Eric Owen born in 1893 and Guy Henry Goad born in 1897.

One of the few photographs of Mr J J Crosfield Chairman of the Board of Management – sitting on the left of Miss B Stevens, Matron. On her right are Mr Stanley Bower, Dr Selby, Sister Davies and Sister Mather.

After working in the family firm for many years, he became Managing Director in 1906. During these years he successfully resisted attempts by Lever Brothers to take over Crosfield Ltd and maintained the continued growth of the company. In July 1915 he resigned his directorship after a dispute with the Board. During this period he had a number of local interests. Early in the same year he had become Chairman of the Management Board of Frodsham Auxiliary Military Hospital, which undertaking must have taken up a good deal of his time.

Like so many parents during the War years, Joseph and his wife had to suffer the loss of their second son, Guy Henry, who was killed at the battle of Passchendaele in 1917. There is a memorial tablet to his memory in St Laurence Church, Frodsham.

After the War, Mr and Mrs Crosfield moved to Embley Park – Florence Nightingale's' former home – near Romsey in Hampshire. During his retirement, he served on various local committees and became High Sheriff of Southampton in 1932.

Joseph Crosfield was extremely generous to several charities. Among the gifts he made were £10,000 to Warrington Infirmary and £10,000 to King Edward's Hospital Fund. Without a doubt, he must have contributed sums to the hospital at Overton whilst, at the same time, working hard and very ably as Chairman of the Board.

'Netherdale'.
The house in Carriage Drive, Frodsham – built for Joseph Crosfield in 1892.

Chapter 5 — FROM BATTLEFIELD TO BLIGHTY

TRANSPORT AND CARE OF THE WOUNDED

Casualties were brought from the trenches in Northern France and Belgium to the ports, where they were transferred to the south coast of England in hospital ships. Many of the wounded were taken to the Casualty Clearing Station at Eastleigh, near Southampton. From there they were sent by train to their various destinations, for example, Chester. At Chester Station they were met by ambulances or motor cars, which transported them to the auxiliary hospitals in the area, one of which was Frodsham Auxiliary Military Hospital.

The Casualty Clearing Station at Eastleigh had been established in April 1915. The purpose of this medical unit was to receive direct from the hospital ships the men who, in civil hospitals, would be classed as outpatients. These were the ones who were not too seriously wounded or ill and, therefore, did not require special accommodation in ambulance trains. The casualties were sifted at Eastleigh and sent to other hospitals by ordinary passenger trains or discharged as 'fit for duty' after two or three weeks' stay in the Clearing Station. The following report appeared in the *Chester Chronicle* one day in May 1915:

> "*At 4.30 in the morning 52 more wounded soldiers arrived at Chester General Station in a hospital train. The "disembarkation" scenes have so often been described in our columns that we need only say that the men were carefully and expeditiously removed to the various hospitals. They were all tired and feeling the effects of their long journey.*"

According to the report, the numbers of men sent to the various auxiliary hospitals were:

Richmond House	7
Hoole Bank	8
Frodsham	25
Vernon Institute, Saughall	6
Eaton Hall	5
Ledsham	4
Helsby	2
Bunbury	3
Ashton Hayes	2

The fact that a relatively large number of patients were despatched to Frodsham suggests that there were surplus beds at the Overton hospital in the spring, as well as later in the year.

Another report in the *Chester Chronicle*, this time for 8 May 1915, gives more detail of how the men reached Frodsham and how they were treated upon arrival at Overton:

"They came from Southampton during the day, their train carrying over 300 wounded and sick soldiers. A number of Frodsham people lent their motor cars, and in these the 30 cases were conveyed to Frodsham. All the casualties were sitting-up cases, and the ambulance was not required. The local ambulance men were present, however, and assisted in preparing the patients for their beds, under the superintendence of Doctors Ellison, Selby and Burton, and the hospital staff. By 8 o'clock all the soldiers were comfortably tucked-up in bed, very thankful to have reached such homely quarters after continuous travelling practically since Wednesday."

The reporter adds this interesting piece of information, which confirms statements made earlier about the number of beds at Overton in the first few months:

"Eleven patients were still in, so the number of inmates now receiving attention is 41. The total accommodation being for 50 cases. The majority of the latest batch are suffering from bullet and shrapnel wounds, but none of them very serious."

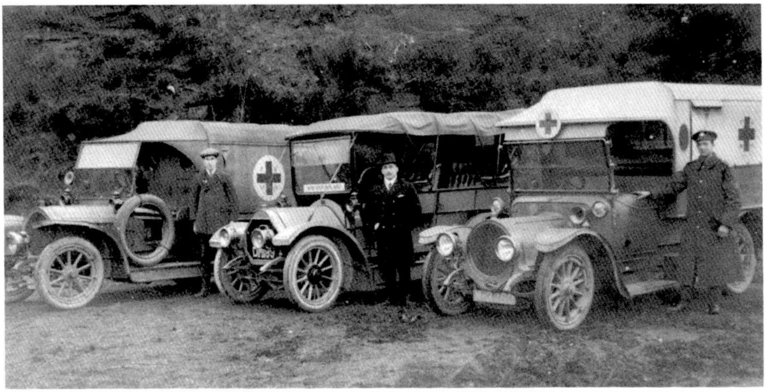

Fleet of ambulances parked near the hospital.
Mr Stanley Bower (centre) with Sgt Bill Simmons (right).

Reports of the wounded men arriving at Chester Station appear regularly in the local newspapers throughout the years. One of the most graphic accounts was published in the *Chester Chronicle* on Saturday 8 July 1916. The train from Southampton steamed into Chester at 9 o'clock. The large crowd which had gathered at the station approaches cheered the wounded men as they were brought through to the waiting cars and ambulances. The reporter describes the scene as follows:

"Mud-stained and torn tunics told how the men had come straight from the trenches. Crippled limbs and bandaged bodies showed their suffering. The walking-wounded moved first and then the stretcher cases.

In this instance, Frodsham received 24 patients, including six cot cases.

THE PATIENTS

According to the official statistics, patients stayed at Overton for an average of 36.6 days. So, it would appear that they were rehabilitated fairly quickly. Although from the photographs it is evident that a number of the men had amputated limbs, these operations almost certainly took place prior to their arrival at Frodsham. However, there was a small operating theatre at the hospital and a certain amount of surgery was carried out there on a regular basis.

Joseph Brereton, whose family lived in Francis Road, Frodsham served his time as a gas fitter. During the First World War he was sent to the hospital once a week, or the time of an emergency, to ensure that the gas appliances (water boiler etc) were in good working order during operations.

Evidence suggests that, though some of the patients were confined to bed for a while, many were in reasonable health and enjoying a period of convalescence.

The following report from the *Chester Chronicle* for June 1916 gives a rare glimpse of a typical scene at the Overton hospital:

> "*Our representative visited the hospital on Wednesday afternoon and found a number of the returned warriors enjoying the fresh air in the splendidly elevated grounds surrounding the hospital, and the view to be obtained was very different from the view which has met their eyes continually for the past few months! Inside, the hospital was most cheery, and visiting day helped to enliven the hours. A splendid array of flowers sent by the kindly disposed Frodsham people were artistically arranged in all parts of the commodious ward. Some of the soldiers were in bed, others – reading, some writing, others enjoying themselves in the recreation room.*"

The reporter goes on to heap praise on Frodsham people for their unstinting support for the hospital:

> "*The Frodsham people do not do things by halves, and in fitting-up the hospital and lavishing gifts upon it day-by-day, have been most thoughtful and generous. Two Chester men spoke highly of their treatment, and said it was quite a treat after all they had gone through. One of them described "the whole business" (i.e., the war) as nothing but murder on a large scale.*"

Cigarettes and Tobacco

One ironic feature of the provisions for patients – in the light of modern medical knowledge – is the allowance of cigarettes. Since the hospital opened, all the patients were provided with ten cigarettes a day, or the equivalent in smoking tobacco, and a box of matches. One wonders if smoking was allowed in the wards or if it was restricted to only certain places and certain times of the day.

Entertainment

A healthier pastime, which patients enjoyed, was the weekly shows provided by the Entertainment Committee. In 1917, the Committee had three members: Mrs Hutchings, Mrs Bury and Mrs Glover. In December of that year they decided to hold a 'sale' to raise funds to help with the expense of running these shows. The event was to be held on Wednesday 5 December at 2 pm at 'Eversley', the home of Mr and Mrs Bury. Many people must have contributed generously, as there were valuable items of needlework, china, glass and other antiques for sale. Unfortunately, there is no record of how many people attended and how much money was raised.

Uniforms

All soldiers in military hospitals were required to wear the regulation dress supplied by the War Office. The patients at Overton wore a bright blue uniform with red collars and cuffs and white lapels. The standard footwear was brown boots. The other essential part of the uniform was a red tie but the soldiers were allowed to wear their own regimental caps – as can be seen below:

This photograph, from May 1917, shows a range of patients' injuries. Beds have been carried to the cleared ground outside Ward III.

Maintaining Discipline

In addition to difficulties arising from the patients' medical needs, a set of problems facing the hospital authorities was that concerned with the upholding of discipline, especially among the convalescents. Although all the men would be still subject to military discipline, it would not be so easy to enforce in the more relaxed atmosphere of such an institution. From the few records that remain of the Overton hospital, it is not easy to ascertain what the rules of daily living were, but it must have been necessary, for example, for the able-bodied patients to observe certain times for meals, for medical treatment and for lights out at night. When the convalescent patients were allowed to leave the premises, they would have to follow certain standards of behaviour and observe a curfew in the evening.

One of the few references to hospital discipline occurs in a report, which appeared in the Chester Chronicle for Saturday 17 June 1916. A case concerning a woman who lived in Ship Street, Frodsham had come before the local magistrates. On a certain evening, two soldiers from the auxiliary hospital were seen going into her house and, shortly afterwards, she went to purchase beer from the Red Lion.

She was charged with having procured beer for two soldiers who were undergoing treatment at the Frodsham hospital. Mr Stanley Bower, the Officer-in-Charge, said that practically the only breaches of discipline were caused through drink. The magistrate stated that it was “cruel” of the woman to tempt the men in this way, as any misdemeanours committed by the soldiers under the influence of drink could result in severe military punishment. The magistrate decided that the woman should be fined 20 shillings or serve 14 days imprisonment.

In the logbook of the auxiliary hospital established in Ramsgate and staffed by Kent VAD, there are a number of references to patients being “sent away”, usually for drunkenness or failure to observe the curfew. In some instances, unruly patients were sent to nearby regular military hospitals, where they would be subject to stricter discipline.

Unfortunately, there is no record of any similar logbook for the Overton hospital, but it is reasonable to assume that this kind of problems arose there too, and that they were dealt with along the same lines.

SUPPLIES TO THE HOSPITAL

In most parts of the country, basic food supplies were sent to auxiliary hospitals from county depots and, as far as we know, this is what happened in Frodsham. However, undoubtedly, certain provisions, such as dairy products and fresh fruit, were obtained locally. One example of this practice was foodstuffs purchased from the 'Berringtons'. Mary Ann Berrington, a young woman, became a cook at the hospital. Her parents kept a smallholding off Bellemonte Road – with three or four cows, pigs and hens. During the War years, soldiers were regularly sent to collect eggs and milk for the hospital kitchens.

SOLDIERS FROM OVERSEAS

Although the majority of patients at Overton were serving with the British regiments, a few were from distant parts of the British Empire. A number of Australian soldiers can be seen in the photographs – often recognised by their distinctive caps – and men from Canada are also mentioned in the records. One other unique piece of evidence has come to light recently: a small slab of sandstone (photograph below) showing the cleverly carved face of a soldier and round the edge is the inscription:

"OVERTON HOSP WOUNDED 1914-18 AUSTRALIA".

A carving of an Australian patient on sandstone, probably a self-portrait.

Was this the only stone of its kind ever made the hospital or, at some stage, were there groups of men busy making sculptures in stone or wood – not only as a record of their stay, but also as a recreational activity?

Right of stove: Private Mundy, Private Harbar (with bandaged head), Nurse Cameron, Privates Johnson and Rutledge (Australian soldiers).
Sitting, left: Privates Evans, Smith and Fell.
Sitting, right: Sergeants Clarke and Gibbs and Private Samson.

Nurse Cameron, Sister Davies, Sister Mather, 'Hughie' and Nurse Urmson with patients in Ward II – Christmas 1918.

Sister Mather in Ward II – Christmas 1917.
The patients in the background are probably having a meal.

From left: Privates Mundy, Evans, Pilling, Fell and Howgood.
May be the same men having a meal as in the photograph above.
Judging by the amount of steam, the food was piping hot!

Privates Tranter and O'Rourke – two Australian soldiers.

Privates Neyland, Harbar, Hopwood, Banks, Day, Nutting and Welsby outside Ward III – February 1918.

Patients outside the office building that was converted into a private dwelling by George Aitken in later years.

Medicines and Dressings trolley.
(Bed on left has a frame for traction.)

Back, left: Private Pycroft.
Front: Privates Tommy Atkinson and Hough.

Enjoying the Summer – August 1917.
Back: Pte Spalding, Sgt Case, Pte Rich, Pte Tormey and Pte Stevens.
Front: Pte Saregan, Sgt Moor and Pte Barton.

Patients, including three bed cases, enjoying fresh air outside Ward II June 1917.

Pte Pickup and Pte Rundle (back) and
Pte Martin and Pte Orr (front, middle).

Front, from left: Privates Lunsden, Bowler and Williams and Sgt Moon.
Back, from left: Privates Saregan, Edmunds, Toomey, Buckle and Cormack.
Middle of the group: Sister Davies.

Nurse De Silva (2nd row, 2nd from right) with a colleague and patients outside Ward III.

Nurse De Silva with another group of patients. (Probably September 1917.)

Nurses Dorothea Urmson (left) and two colleagues.
(Many of the photographs in this book are from Nurse Urmson's album.)

Nurses and patients in fancy dress with Mr Bower and Matron (centre) - Christmas 1918.

Chapter 6 — Stories of a Few Individual Patients

The First Arrivals

In one of the first batches of wounded men to arrive at the Frodsham Auxiliary Military Hospital was **Corporal W H Youd** whose family lived at the Bear's Paw Hotel in Main Street. Cpl Youd had been attached to the Army Service Corps in France as a despatch rider. One day he suffered an injury to his foot and then, whilst on the ambulance wagon, he came under shellfire and received a nasty wound in the thigh. He arrived at the hospital early in June 1915 and, as far as we know, made good recovery.

Another Frodsham man at the hospital in these early days was **Arnold Lightfoot** of the Guards, who was wounded in November 1914. After receiving treatment in various hospitals, he was sent home to recuperate. However, his wound did not heal and, so, after X-ray examination, the medical staff decided to remove pieces of bone from his hip. This was done and he made a slow recovery.

Australians at Overton

Miss Mary Gold tells the remarkable story of how two of her Australian relatives came to be patients at the hospital. Samuel Moreton, an ancestor of hers, emigrated to Melbourne in 1853. He had intended to take up farming but managed to set-up in the more lucrative business of selling boots to gold diggers. A few years later he married and eventually had five sons and two daughters.

Three of his sons fought in the Gallipoli campaign. After a time at the battlefront, one was killed but the other two were wounded and sent to a military hospital in Manchester. On hearing of their arrival, John Davies cycled to Manchester, found the boys and asked for them to be transferred to Frodsham, where their relatives could visit them. The request was granted and they were duly moved to the Overton hospital.

The Davies Family

The Davies family had a further connection with the hospital. For a time, both mother and daughter served there as volunteer nurses. Sadly, Algernon died of his wounds on 27 October 1918 whilst in action with the Cheshire Regiment in West Flanders.

The photograph (see next page) shows Mrs Davies with her five sons and her daughter.

Family of John Gifford Davies of Brook House, Main Street, Frodsham. From left: Don, Algernon, Elsie, Herbert, Colin and Bert, with (seated) Edith Ellen, their mother.

Ambulance Driver

Another story of a former patient of the hospital was told by the late Mrs Lyons of Bellemonte Road. Her father, **Mr Bill Simmons** of Bexhill-on-Sea, was serving with his regiment on the Western Front until the almost inevitable happened and he was wounded in battle. By chance, he was sent to the Overton hospital. When he had recovered sufficiently, he became an ambulance driver there. After the closure of the hospital in 1919, he decided to settle in Frodsham.

During this time, the ambulances were kept at Overton Hall, the home of Mr T Stanley Bower, who also provided facilities for nurses at No 95 Bellemonte Road. These premises not only provided some of the nurses with accommodation, but also a rest place for them to use during their off-day periods.

Private Ellison

A Canadian visitor to Frodsham in 1999 related the story of how his father came to be a patient at the Overton hospital. Harry Ellison had joined the Cheshire Regiment in the early part of the War and 'celebrated' his twenty-first birthday on 19 June 1916 during the Battle of the Somme. Having survived that ordeal, his regiment was in the thick of fighting at Passchendaele in 1917.

One day, during an advance, he was moving slowly forward with five or six of his comrades, when one of them suggested that they should stop for a bite to eat. They rested in an abandoned German bunker. Suddenly, an enemy shell hit the roof above their heads. A large block of concrete came crashing down on top of him. In the turmoil and havoc of the battlefield, he was left for dead. Miraculously, he was found later by medical corps personnel, who rescued him from No Man's Land.

His wounds were so extensive that in later life he could never recall where he was taken or what treatment he received. Finally, he was brought by train to Chester and then by Red Cross ambulance to Overton. It fell to Dr Selby to inform his mother that her son was a patient at the hospital. Unfortunately, little is known of his stay except that, because of his extensive wounds, he remained confined to bed.

One interesting detail has emerged, however. Namely, that the patients were visited on a regular basis by a group of ladies who encouraged the men to try some needlework. Over a period of months, Harry Ellison learnt to stitch sufficiently well to produce a fine embroidery of his Regimental Badge.

Harry Ellison's embroidery of his Regimental Badge, completed whilst convalescing at Frodsham hospital.

After a few months at Overton, Pte Ellison was transferred to another hospital – in Maghull. He was finally discharged in November 1918. Despite his lengthy treatment, his health remained poor and Dr Selby advised him to escape from the cold, damp climate of England by emigrating. After finishing his time as an apprentice carpenter, he decided to follow his girl-friend to Canada. She had left with her parents a few years previously to join relatives in Winnipeg. Harry arrived in Canada in 1923 and married his fiancée in 1925.

Private Harry Ellison (2nd row, 1st left) with comrades from Cheshire Regiment on the Western Front in 1916.

PRIVATE FRED LEWIS

Another intriguing story with a Canadian connection is that of Fred Lewis who became a patient at Overton hospital during the First World war. Fred was born in London, the son of a Thames River worker. He had an unhappy childhood and emigrated to Canada with a friend and his family at the age of about 14 years. He worked until the War broke out, and then joined the Canadian Army. After a while, he was posted to France where, like so many others, he was wounded. By chance, he was sent to convalesce at the Frodsham hospital. During his stay, he was invited to have tea with the Lawless family – the well-known Frodsham bakers. There he was introduced to Elsie Lloyd, who was in service with the family and, through her, he met Annie, her sister. This marked the start of their courtship.

After a time, Fred went back to his regiment but continued to write to Annie. After the War he returned to Canada, found a job, bought a house and sent for Annie to join him. She sailed alone to Montreal and they married in London, Ontario in 1920.

Pte Fred Lewis (2nd row, 2nd right – next to soldier with arm in sling).

'Home from the "Push"' almost certainly meant that these men had been injured in the Battle of the Somme in July 1916.

The tents on the right are probably some of those issued by the Army, but quickly returned as surplus to requirement.

SERGEANT MAJOR FINNERTY

John Patrick Finnerty, whose family came from Ireland, was born in Birkenhead c.1893. In 1912 he signed on as a regular soldier and eventually became a Sgt Major in the King's Horse Artillery. After the outbreak of the War, he fought on the Western Front for about two years before he was wounded. As a result of his injuries he lost two or three ribs. Also, he had one of his fingers shot away. At the same time he began to suffer terribly from shell shock. After returning to England, he was sent to a military hospital in Shropshire and then to Frodsham for more convalescence.

Whilst at Overton, Sgt Major Finnerty met his future wife. After a few weeks, he became friendly with one of the nurses, Violet May Webb, and soon their romance blossomed. They were married at St Laurence Church in 1919. They lived at 91 Main Street, Frodsham and, in due course, they had a family of two children.

Private Tindle

Pte John W Tindle served in the 4th Dorset Regiment. His service number was 23261. He was wounded on active service and spent some time recovering at Overton. In May 1918 he sent the photograph of himself (see below) to the Matron and staff of the hospital. On the back he wrote:

> "*In grateful remembrance of your kindness during my stay at the Frodsham Auxiliary Military Hospital. With best wishes, J W Tindle, May 1918*"

Private Tindle

LANCE CORPORAL ALBERT WORRALL

Born in March 1899, Albert Worrall of Rake Lane, Helsby enlisted on 12 April 1917. After training with the Manchesters, he transferred to the Notts and Derbyshire Regiment. Later in the year he was sent to the front line in Flanders.

Towards the end of May 1918, a shell destroyed his section. He and one other man were the only survivors. Badly wounded in both legs, L/Cpl Worrall was taken prisoner by German troops.

German doctors operated on his legs immediately. Much to his relief, the operation was successful and he began the slow and painful process of recovery. Conditions in the POW camp were grim and L/Cpl Worrall complained for years afterwards about the poor diet which, he used to say, did him more harm than the German shell.

Shortly after the Armistice of November 1918, he was given his release and eventually he arrived at the Frodsham Auxiliary Military Hospital where he continued his slow convalescence. One of the things upon which he often remarked in later life was how the 'Thousand Steps' (between Bellemonte Hotel and the top end of Overton village) presented him with quite a challenge on his crutches.

Lance Corporal Worrall (left) with a comrade during his time at FAMH. (the hospital uniforms can just be seen under their great coats.)

WAR GRAVES

Most patients were nursed back to health, but those who died were either buried in St Laurence Churchyard, Frodsham or at a cemetery in their home town. As far as we know, all these soldiers were buried with full military honours. Of the ten War Graves in the Frodsham churchyard, three are those of men who died at the Overton hospital. They were: Pte Alfred Ernest Carter of the Leicestershire Regiment, whose funeral was described earlier (see pages 27-28); Pte Frederick George Price of the King's Shropshire Light Infantry who died on 2 August 1916 of wounds received in action; and finally, Pte George McKay, a Canadian soldier, who died on 17 November 1918, aged 24 years. His regimental details are given as 712371, 78th Battalion, Canadian Infantry.

Private McKay's grave in St Laurence Churchyard, Frodsham.

Private Ridgeway and Corporal Taylor

In addition to the three deaths mentioned above, a few more patients died at the hospital but they were buried elsewhere. Two soldiers in this category were Pte Ridgeway and Cpl Taylor.

Pte Ridgeway of the 3rd London died on Friday 9 November 1917. He had been at the hospital for six months, suffering from wounds in the back that developed into septic poisoning. His home was in Manchester.

Cpl Taylor of the Royal Field Artillery died on 21 August 1917. He was 35 years old and came from Southport. He was wounded in action on 7 August, tetanus set in and death resulted. His burial took place at Southport Cemetery.

Chapter 7 — Closure and the Aftermath

A Tribute from Joseph Crosfield

Frodsham Auxiliary Military Hospital closed in September 1919. In a statement accompanying the presentation of the final accounts in January 1920, Joseph Crosfield, the Chairman of the Board of Management explained that it had been kept open long after the end of the War for the treatment of pensioners. As a result, there had been no formal closing of the hospital and no opportunity to present the final accounts or to thank those who had served it so well: notably the Officer-in-Charge, the doctors, the Matron and the staff, the honorary Treasurer and the Honorary Secretary.

He went on to say that the accounts, which he was now presenting, did not show the true value of the contribution from the townspeople as the value of gifts – other than money – and the voluntary services rendered were not included. If these services were taken into account, the total value of all contributions would far exceed £15,000. As it was, the total figure for donations stood at £7,155.0s.3d (see Appendix 1 for Statement of Accounts for March 1915 to September 1919).

Mr Crosfield added that since the hospital opened, 3,435 men had passed through it and the total number of patient-days, i.e., the total number of days the men had spent in the hospital, amounted to 156,292.

He concluded that the excellent work done by the hospital was shown not only by the accounts, but also by gratitude of the patients and by the "*well-merited decorations bestowed upon the Office-in-Charge, the Matron and the various members of staff. Altogether, it is a record of which Frodsham may look back with pride*".

Finally he added: "*It was a fine example of what can be accomplished by all working together for the common good*".

A Fine Memorial

In Chester Cathedral, there is a special memorial to all the First World War auxiliary hospitals in Cheshire. On the wall of the Consistory Court is a beautifully made banner commemorating the voluntary work of the doctors, nurses and other staff who performed their duties faithfully during those difficult years.

As the photograph (overleaf) shows, the banner depicts the badges of St John's Ambulance Association and British Red Cross on a background of the Tudor Rose, Scottish Thistle, Irish Shamrock and Welsh Leek. In the border is the Tree of Life and in its branches are the badges of all the regiments in which the sick and wounded soldiers served. The Arms of England, Scotland, Ireland and Wales are shown in the four corners. At the top of the border are a silver dove and the rays of the Holy Spirit. The dove and the regimental badges were embroidered by disabled soldiers.

The Banner in the Consistory Court, Chester Cathedral.

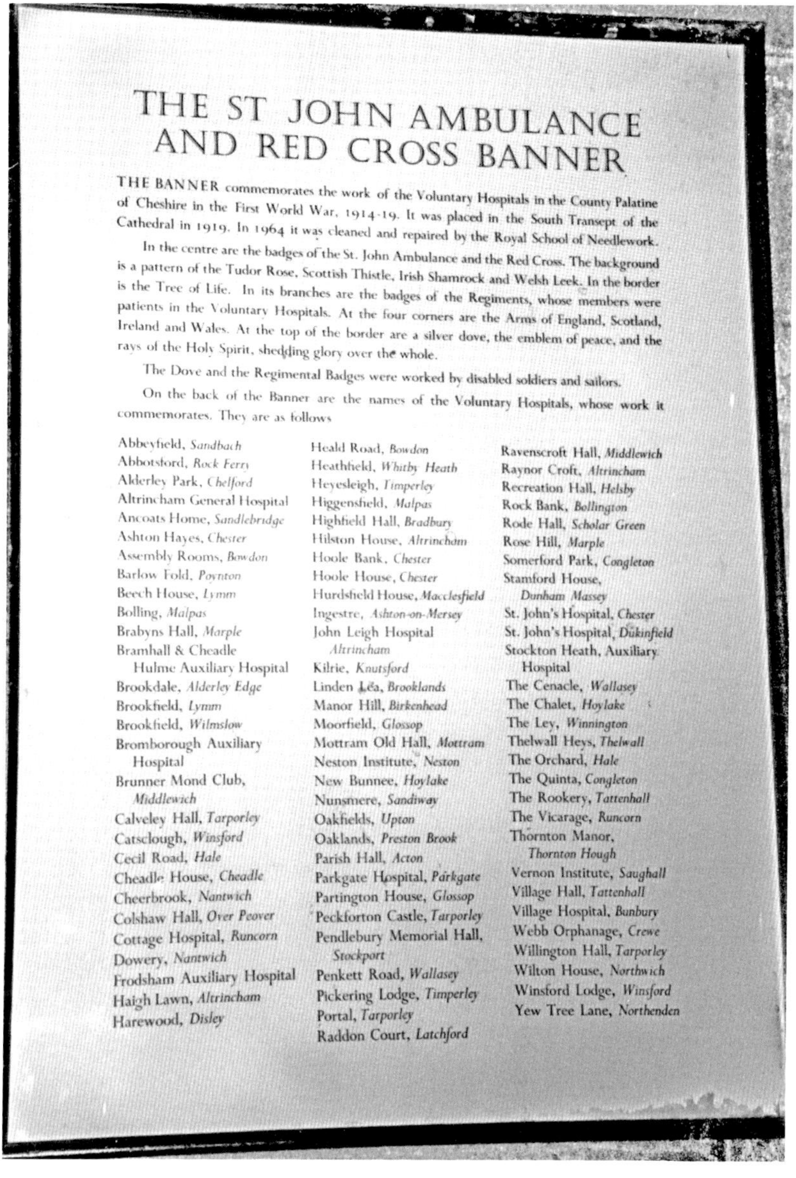
THE ST JOHN AMBULANCE AND RED CROSS BANNER

THE BANNER commemorates the work of the Voluntary Hospitals in the County Palatine of Cheshire in the First World War, 1914-19. It was placed in the South Transept of the Cathedral in 1919. In 1964 it was cleaned and repaired by the Royal School of Needlework.

In the centre are the badges of the St. John Ambulance and the Red Cross. The background is a pattern of the Tudor Rose, Scottish Thistle, Irish Shamrock and Welsh Leek. In the border is the Tree of Life. In its branches are the badges of the Regiments, whose members were patients in the Voluntary Hospitals. At the four corners are the Arms of England, Scotland, Ireland and Wales. At the top of the border are a silver dove, the emblem of peace, and the rays of the Holy Spirit, shedding glory over the whole.

The Dove and the Regimental Badges were worked by disabled soldiers and sailors.

On the back of the Banner are the names of the Voluntary Hospitals, whose work it commemorates. They are as follows

Abbeyfield, *Sandbach*
Abbotsford, *Rock Ferry*
Alderley Park, *Chelford*
Altrincham General Hospital
Ancoats Home, *Sandlebridge*
Ashton Hayes, *Chester*
Assembly Rooms, *Bowdon*
Barlow Fold, *Poynton*
Beech House, *Lymm*
Bolling, *Malpas*
Brabyns Hall, *Marple*
Bramhall & Cheadle Hulme Auxiliary Hospital
Brookdale, *Alderley Edge*
Brookfield, *Lymm*
Brookfield, *Wilmslow*
Bromborough Auxiliary Hospital
Brunner Mond Club, *Middlewich*
Calveley Hall, *Tarporley*
Catsclough, *Winsford*
Cecil Road, *Hale*
Cheadle House, *Cheadle*
Cheerbrook, *Nantwich*
Colshaw Hall, *Over Peover*
Cottage Hospital, *Runcorn*
Dowery, *Nantwich*
Frodsham Auxiliary Hospital
Haigh Lawn, *Altrincham*
Harewood, *Disley*
Heald Road, *Bowdon*
Heathfield, *Whitby Heath*
Heyesleigh, *Timperley*
Higgensfield, *Malpas*
Highfield Hall, *Bradbury*
Hilston House, *Altrincham*
Hoole Bank, *Chester*
Hoole House, *Chester*
Hurdsfield House, *Macclesfield*
Ingestre, *Ashton-on-Mersey*
John Leigh Hospital *Altrincham*
Kilrie, *Knutsford*
Linden Lea, *Brooklands*
Manor Hill, *Birkenhead*
Moorfield, *Glossop*
Mottram Old Hall, *Mottram*
Neston Institute, *Neston*
New Bunnee, *Hoylake*
Nunsmere, *Sandiway*
Oakfields, *Upton*
Oaklands, *Preston Brook*
Parish Hall, *Acton*
Parkgate Hospital, *Parkgate*
Partington House, *Glossop*
Peckforton Castle, *Tarporley*
Pendlebury Memorial Hall, *Stockport*
Penkett Road, *Wallasey*
Pickering Lodge, *Timperley*
Portal, *Tarporley*
Raddon Court, *Latchford*
Ravenscroft Hall, *Middlewich*
Raynor Croft, *Altrincham*
Recreation Hall, *Helsby*
Rock Bank, *Bollington*
Rode Hall, *Scholar Green*
Rose Hill, *Marple*
Somerford Park, *Congleton*
Stamford House, *Dunham Massey*
St. John's Hospital, *Chester*
St. John's Hospital, *Dukinfield*
Stockton Heath, Auxiliary Hospital
The Cenacle, *Wallasey*
The Chalet, *Hoylake*
The Ley, *Winnington*
Thelwall Heys, *Thelwall*
The Orchard, *Hale*
The Quinta, *Congleton*
The Rookery, *Tattenhall*
The Vicarage, *Runcorn*
Thornton Manor, *Thornton Hough*
Vernon Institute, *Saughall*
Village Hall, *Tattenhall*
Village Hospital, *Bunbury*
Webb Orphanage, *Crewe*
Willington Hall, *Tarporley*
Wilton House, *Northwich*
Winsford Lodge, *Winsford*
Yew Tree Lane, *Northenden*

On the back of the banner are the names of all the voluntary hospitals in Cheshire, including the Frodsham Auxiliary Military Hospital.

T STANLEY BOWER, OBE

After the First World War, Mr Bower and Miss Stevens, Matron of the Overton hospital opened a nursing home at Gamber Terrace – opposite the Anglican Cathedral, Liverpool.

As stated above, Mr T Stanley Bower lived at Overton Hall, Five Crosses, Frodsham. He was the director of a Liverpool firm engaged in the coastal shipping business. After the war he became Chairman of the Prince of Wales Hotel Co Ltd, Southport and a Director of the Overton Steamship Company.

He and his wife had one daughter, Elsa, who married Mr Anthony Horner, whose father worked as an engineer for the Manchester Ship Canal Company. The young couple went out to Tanganyika (now Tanzania), where Mr Horner worked as a dock construction engineer at Daar-as-Salaam.

Stanley Bower had always had a keen interest in local affairs and he became President of the Frodsham Conservative Club and Chairman of the Frodsham Committee of the Eddisbury Divisional Conservative Association during the 1920s. A founder member of the Frodsham and District Agricultural and Horticultural Society, he served as its Chairman for many years. Also, he had become a prominent Freemason and was a member of several Lodges.

According to the writer of his obituary in the *Chester Chronicle*, he was "*a generous supporter of all the local churches and chapels. No one appealed in vain for his support to any deserving cause*".

In the early 1930s he helped to establish a centre for the unemployed at Castle Park. Perhaps, his greatest achievement was during the War when, as we have seen, he was chiefly instrumental in inaugurating Frodsham Auxiliary Military Hospital.

To quote again from his obituary: "*It was through his leadership and beneficence that it became recognised as one of the best equipped medical institutions of its kind in the country*".

He served as the Officer-in-Charge at FAMH for four-and-a-half years, and it was in recognition of these services that Mar Bower was awarded the OBE in 1919.

He died in 1935 aged 70 and was buried at Southport Cemetery.

Overton Hall, Five Crosses, Frodsham.
Formerly the home of Mr T Stanley Bower, OBE.

No 95 Bellemonte Road, Frodsham.
The house at which Mr Bower provided rest and recreation facilities for nurses in their off-duty periods.

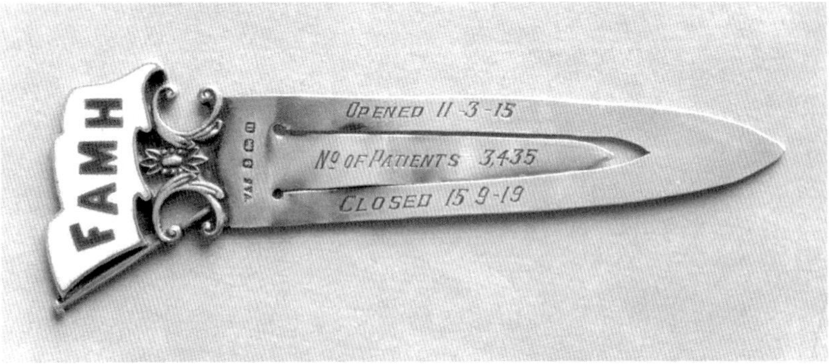

Commemorative silver bookmark.
The managers gave one of these to every member of staff shortly after the hospital closed in September 1919.

Some of the houses built on former hospital site.
Pictured in 2001.

Four generations of the family that played a major part in the development of Mersey View and Bellemonte Recreation Grounds.

Mrs Parker Hoose (right); Mrs Annie Bate, daughter (on her right); Mrs Zillah Sampson, granddaughter (left) and Juliet, Zillah's daughter (front).

Photographed on 17 October 1923 at the wedding of George Aitken and Millicent Bate.

The bungalow in the background was used as an office in the days of the hospital.

Fate of the Buildings

After it closed down as an auxiliary military hospital in September 1919, the premises never reverted to their former use – as a roller-skating park. Concerts and dances, including carnival balls, were held in the main hall during the 1920s, but late in the 1930s it ceased to be used for entertainment.

At the same time Mr George Aitken made use of some of the buildings. He converted the former office premises, which stood in front of the entrance to the main hall, into a dwelling and, from that time onwards, it was generally known as George Aitken's bungalow. The building which had the glass-panelled doors (Ward III) became his garage, where he kept a couple of wagons and a charabanc. In the 1930s he ran regular charabanc trips to Liverpool and North Wales.

During the Second World War, the hall was requisitioned by the government and it became a depot for the Ministry of Food.

In the 1960s, the former hospital premises were used by the late Mr Alan Oultram for his heating business but eventually, the firm moved to a more convenient site.

The remaining buildings were demolished to make way for private premises in 1984.

The Maple Floor

Some years ago, the late Mrs Beb Savage told the following remarkable story:

> *"A few years after the War, representatives of an American company visiting Frodsham were so intrigued with the quality of this sprung maple floor that they decided to buy a large part of it. After carefully numbering each piece, it was taken up and sent to Pennsylvania, where it was re-laid in a Pittsburgh ten-pin bowling alley. By co-incidence, my brother-in-law lived in Pittsburgh and when I was visiting him some years later, someone mentioned this connection with Frodsham. When the owners were told, I was invited to view the floor and walk on a 'little bit of Frodsham' in the USA."*

Mrs Savage said how thrilled she had been to see it and to read a small plaque on the wall which stated that this fine maple floor came from a former military hospital in Frodsham, England.

In Conclusion

Although there were those who said that Bellemonte was an inconvenient location for a hospital, the site on the slopes of Overton Hill must have been, in many ways, idyllic, especially in summer time. For the thousands of soldiers returning from the Somme, Mons, Ypres and other battlefields of Northern France and Belgium, the rural tranquillity of Overton provided a wonderful rehabilitation centre.

As we have seen, it became a sizeable establishment and it served its intended purpose extremely well. Certainly, the 3,435 patients who recovered their health at Overton were glad of the treatment they received there. Many, if not all, went away with fond memories of Frodsham Auxiliary Military Hospital.

Bibliography

British Red Cross – Accounts for Auxiliary Military Hospitals – 1918

British Red Cross – Cheshire Branch Report and Accounts for the Year 1919

Cynthia O'Neill - "*A Picture of Health – Hospitals and Nursing in Old Picture Postcards*" - Meadow Books – 1991

Major-General Sir W G Macpherson - "*Medical Services General History*" Volume 1 – 1919

Vera Brittain - "*Testament of Youth*" Virago Press – 1978

Thekla Bowker - "*The Story of British VAD Work in the Great War*" Melrose, London – 1918

F W Longbottom - "*Chester in the Great War*" - 1920

George D Mealor - "*An Unorthodox History of Oaklands*" - 1923

Paul Creswick et al - "*Kent's Care for the Wounded*" Hodder and Stoughton – 1915

Frodsham parish Magazines – 1915-1919

Chester Chronicle – 1915-1919

Runcorn Weekly News – 1915-1919

Hazel Basford – Quex Park Auxiliary Military Hospital – 1914-1919

Log Book of Ramsgate Auxiliary Hospital – Imperial War Museum – Miscellaneous – 2018

APPENDIX I
FRODSHAM AUXILIARY MILITARY HOSPITAL
STATEMENT OF ACCOUNTS TO 31 DECEMBER 1916

Receipts	**£ - s - d**
Subscriptions	2,141 - 18 - 2
Maintenance of Beds	425 - 9 - 4
Concerts	98 - 8 - 0
Workmen's Contribution	393 - 15 - 4
Miscellaneous	163 - 18 - 6
Capitation Grant	6,068 - 7 - 9
	9,291 - 16 - 4

Payments	
Equipment, inc adaptation of original ward and construction of new one	2,303 - 10 - 5
Maintenance of Building and Repairs	517 - 15 - 7
Fuel, Light and Water	432 - 0 - 8
Petty Cash Payments	60 - 0 - 0
Insurance of Buildings and Nurses National Insurance Stamps	36 - 4 - 7
Chemists, Dressings, Drugs, Medicines and Surgical Appliances	604 - 5 - 11
Salaries, Wages and Nurses' Home	932 - 15 - 2
Provisions	3,393 - 0 - 11
Laundries	574 - 10 - 2
Printing, Advertising and Stationery	36 - 13 - 6
Postage and Travelling Expenses	57 - 13 - 5
Newspapers	9 - 0 - 11
Rates and Taxes	9 - 12 - 3
Repairs and Furniture	2 - 14 - 9
Rent	18 - 15 - 0
X-ray Treatment	12 - 2 - 0
Massage	23 - 5 - 0
Miscellaneous	51 - 7 - 8
Balance in Hand	**9,291 - 16 - 4**

STATEMENT OF ACCOUNTS FOR FIVE MONTHS ENDING 31 MAY 1917

Receipts	**£ - s - d**
Balance-in-Hand on 1 Jan 1917	216 - 8 - 5
Donations	243 - 17 - 9
Army Allowance	1,727 - 17 - 0
Farmers' Red Cross Fund (£420-13-7) and Sundry Subs	497 - 14 - 4
Debit Balance	134 - 15 - 2
	2,820 - 12 - 8

Payments	
Maintenance	
Provisions	1,350 - 14 - 10
Surgery and Dispensary	290 - 1 - 9
Domestic	457 - 16 - 4
Establishment	75 - 0 - 9
Salaries and Wages	315 - 19 - 1
Miscellaneous	40 - 1 - 2
Administration	
Management	11 - 4 - 4
Finance – Rent, Rates and Taxes	56 - 15 - 11
Building and Equipment	
Land and Building	200 - 0 - 0
Equipment	22 - 18 - 6
	2,280 - 12 - 8

STATEMENT OF ACCOUNTS FROM THE OPENING OF THE HOSPITAL MARCH 1915 TO CLOSING DATE, SEPTEMBER 1919

		£	s	d
Receipts				
Donations etc		7,155	0	3
Capitation Grants		25,091	8	0
		32,246	**8**	**3**
Deficit		2	7	2
		32,248	**15**	**5**
Expenditure				
Maintenance				
Provisions		15,945	2	8
Surgery and Dispensary		1,972	11	7
Domestic		5,675	11	4
Establishment		1,470	2	0
Salaries and Wages etc		3,925	0	8
Miscellaneous		381	0	10
		29,369	**9**	**1**
Administration				
Management	11 - 4 - 4			
Finance	2 - 0 -10			
		13	5	2
Rents, Rates, Taxes etc		71	9	3
Building and Equipment		2,794	11	11
		32,248	**15**	**5**

(Signed) R H Dutton, Hon Treasurer

Appendix II

War Graves – St Laurence Parish Church, Frodsham

Reference: CRO P8 2619/9/6

I/Leicesters	7614	Private A Carter	died 18/12/1915	E L 4 6
RFA	96911	A/Bdr R Lazenby	died 30/12/15	NE 6 1 7
KSLI	19722	Private F G Price	died 2/8/16	E L 2 1
RDC	25717	Private C Percival	died 9/1/1917	E R 3 3
Cheshires	446	Sgt W Worrall	died 9/5/1917	NE 4 10
RN HMS Canada		Smn L Ellams	died 23/4/1918	NE 3 7
Cheshires	77248	Private A Hopley	died 14/7/1918	NE 3 12
Bn Canadians	712371	Private G McKay	died 17/11/1918	E L 4 3
Cheshires	35080	Private W Massey	died 25/11/1918	NE 2 2
MGC*	64863	Cpl J Bostock	died 9/2/1919	NE 2 10

* MGC = Machine Gun Corp

APPENDIX III
OTHER VOLUNTARY HOSPITALS

The nearest auxiliary hospitals to Frodsham were established at Helsby (see pages 17 and 40), Preston Brook and Runcorn.

Preston Brook

At Preston Brook, Lord Daresbury made available his Victorian mansion, Oaklands and, with the help of the local Red Cross, he organised a hospital there. Oaklands was situated where the Daresbury Park Hotel now stands. In 1918, the hospital had thirty beds and the patients' average residence was 69 days.

Runcorn

During the War, 3,460 servicemen were treated at the Cottage Hospital and at the Parish Church Vicarage Voluntary Hospital, Highlands Road, Runcorn. Cannon Howard Perrin established and ran the latter institution. After the War, he was awarded the OBE for his unfailing endeavours on behalf of the sick and wounded soldiers who were looked after there.

Auxiliary Hospitals in Kent

In Kent, most of the towns and larger villages set-up their own Voluntary Aid Detachments in the years immediately prior to the First World War. The main purpose of these units was to organise auxiliary hospitals and then to provide the staff to man them. In order to prepare themselves for these duties, VAD members attended lectures and engaged in practical work. Sometimes they gained valuable experience by working at a civil or military hospital in the locality.

These units received help and encouragement from their parent body, the British Red Cross or St John's Ambulance Association. After the outbreak of the War, auxiliary hospitals were established in a variety of buildings – parish halls, schools, private houses, disused hotels and even, in one case, at a yacht club. In nearly all instances local residents contributed liberally with money and equipment.

Typical of many small hospitals set-up in Kent is the following:

"KENT 20, TENTERDEN, was started in the town by Mrs Peel at the request of Lady Cranbrook in 1911. The members of the detachment, at first under Dr Skinner as Commandant, have continuously been preparing themselves for any emergency. When mobilised in October 1914, the detachment sent relief to a local hospital until November, when a Red Cross hospital was opened with sixteen beds. This was furnished to a great extent by the local residents who were also most generous in sending contributions. On 30 November 1914, the first party of Belgian soldiers, fifteen in number, arrived." (Page 116, "*Kent Care of the Wounded*" by Paul Creswick and others)

Also by Arthur R Smith

Discovering Mersey View

Discovering Frodsham's Old Schools

The Schools at Overton

The Frodsham Girls' School

William Charles Cotton - Priest, Missionary and Bee Master

Brief Lives - Notable People of Frodsham

Frodsham Town Council Publications

Listed Buildings in Vale Royal

Walks Around Frodsham

The Frodsham Millennium Walks

Frodsham 100 Challenge Walks

Frodsham Parish Paths

Frodsham Town Guide